ZEPHANIAH
BIBLE STUDY GUIDE

ZEPHANIAH
BIBLE STUDY GUIDE

6 EASY-TO-USE STUDIES
FOR GROUPS OR INDIVIDUALS

WITH LEADERS' NOTES
AND SUGGESTED ANSWERS

S K FEATHERSTONE

First published 2023
by The Study Shelf
www.thestudyshelf.co.uk

Editor
Alexa Tewkesbury

British Library Cataloguing-in-Publication Data
A catalogue record for this book is available from
The British Library.

ISBN: 978-1-7395693-0-3
eBook ISBN 978-1-7395693-1-0

THE STUDY SHELF

CONTENTS

ACKNOWLEDGEMENTS

I would like to acknowledge the immense help and support of the following people:

- Alexa Tewkesbury for her scrupulous editing and advice.
- Campbell Patterson for his wisdom and guidance.
- Anne Wardroper, Andrew and Dorothy for their invaluable feedback.
- Graham for encouraging me to get it done!
- My dear friends who have prayed for me.

Most of all, I am grateful to God for His encouragement and provision.

ABOUT THIS STUDY GUIDE

NOTE FROM THE AUTHOR

My prayer is that this study guide will provide a useful tool for you as you explore God's word. You can use it either for personal study or as an off-the-shelf resource for your Bible study group. My intention is that I will have done some of the background work for you.

I have used the NIV Bible throughout. Beware of simplified Bible translations. These may lose a few of the finer details, in which case some questions may not make sense.

USING THIS GUIDE

You will find a mix of questions (marked Q.) and suggested answers (marked A.), together with occasional leaders' notes for more information.

Additional readings throughout the study guide either support the answers given or provide further background information. Use them as part of the study if you have time or perhaps suggest them as extra reading.

Personal Reflections are, as the heading suggests, more personal questions for group members to consider privately and not necessarily to discuss with others.

Space to note down thoughts or answers is included after each question.

GROUP STUDY

If you are a group leader, please tailor the study to your target audience. Re-phrase questions in the way best suited to your group. If you think that a certain question might be inappropriate, feel free to leave it out.

The study is divided into six sessions with the intent that you could cover the whole book of Zephaniah in a typical term.

BEFORE YOUR FIRST SESSION

Encourage everyone to read through Zephaniah and the Introduction to this guide before you begin. Note any questions that arise. Pray!

TIPS FOR PERSONAL STUDY

Read the whole passage without looking at the notes.

What does it say...
- In its time?
- To the Church?
- To you, right now?

What does it not say?
- Are there any widely held beliefs that turn out not to be biblically accurate?
- Have you always thought it said something else?

What stands out for you? Is there anything that surprises you?

INTRODUCTION

Zephaniah's book is among the least-read in the Bible. He himself is one of the twelve minor prophets, but they are not known as 'minor' because they are unimportant. Rather, it's because their books are short. We should not fall into the trap of assuming that they are insignificant and can be ignored, as 2 Timothy 3:16–17 tells us that all scripture is useful and inspired by God. We must look at the book of Zephaniah in the light of that and ask, what does it have to say to us today? If these prophecies are merely historical, why do they remain for us in the Bible? What can we learn?

Studying the Old Testament opens a whole new level of understanding of the New Testament. I would encourage you not to skip over the hidden corners, the seldom-read passages. They are full of illumination and make clear some details that have previously seemed obscure or unimportant.

THEMES

Judgement and Restoration
As with many of the prophets, there is a theme of coming judgement, both for God's people and the surrounding nations, with ultimate restoration for God's faithful people.

The Day of the Lord
Zephaniah has specific prophecies regarding 'The Day of the Lord' for ancient Judah and for the nations and, at the same time, prophecies still to be fulfilled at a future point.

A Future Hope
A brighter future for God's faithful remnant is prophesied.

BACKGROUND

After the death of King Solomon, during the reign of his son Rehoboam, the country was split into two kingdoms: Israel in the north and Judah (including Jerusalem) in the south, as was prophesied to King Solomon.

Q.1 Why was the kingdom divided into two?
Read 1 Kings 11:9–13.

A.1 Solomon's disobedience.

After this, we see a succession of kings, good and bad, and God sends many prophets. Some of the prophets are directed to Israel and others specifically to Judah.

In the middle of the eighth century BC, the kings of Israel have led the people far from God and Hosea the prophet warns of the impending fall of Israel to Assyria. The northern kingdom of Israel falls as prophesied.

The kings of Judah are not much better, swinging from good to bad, with a few notable exceptions such as good kings Hezekiah and Josiah.

King Manasseh

After the reign of King Hezekiah, things went significantly off
the rails for the kingdom of Judah. King Manasseh did evil in
the sight of the Lord. He followed the detestable practices of
the nations that the Lord had previously driven out of the
Promised Land. He rebuilt the high places and erected altars
to Baal. There were many pagan practices in the worship of
false gods; even in the Lord's temple, Manasseh built altars to
the stars. He sacrificed his own son, practised sorcery and
divination and consulted mediums. The Lord was
unsurprisingly provoked to anger.

King Amon

King Manasseh eventually repented, but his son Amon was just
as bad and, by contrast, did not repent. Eventually, Amon was
assassinated, and his son Josiah was made king.

King Josiah

Josiah was very young when he came to the throne (eight
years old) and was under the guardianship of Hilkiah, a priest.
Against the odds, Josiah became a good king and
systematically began purging Judah and Jerusalem of all the
idols and altars to false gods.

During this purge, the book of the Law is found, which
immediately tells a tale of how far the people have strayed
from God's ways. Not only are they not obeying the law but
they don't even know where it has been stashed.

When the book is read to Josiah, he is distraught, tearing his
clothes in remorse at the realisation of how far the nation has
fallen and how angry God must be.

Into this situation comes Zephaniah the prophet. We are not told whether Zephaniah was instrumental in Josiah's reforms, or whether his ministry came later in Josiah's reign.

Additional reading: 2 Chronicles 34: 14–21

A fuller version can be found in 2 Kings 21:1–23:25.

TIMELINE

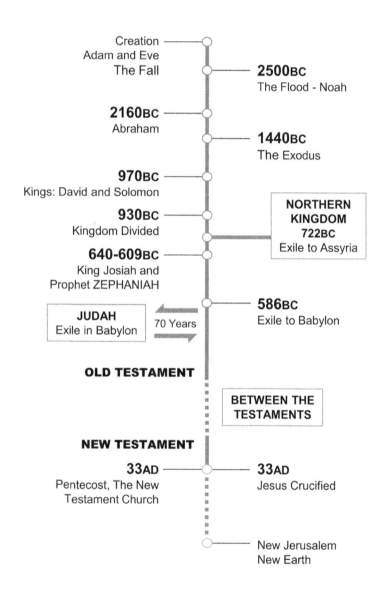

Creation
Adam and Eve
The Fall

2500BC
The Flood - Noah

2160BC
Abraham

1440BC
The Exodus

970BC
Kings: David and Solomon

930BC
Kingdom Divided

NORTHERN KINGDOM 722BC
Exile to Assyria

640-609BC
King Josiah and
Prophet ZEPHANIAH

586BC
Exile to Babylon

JUDAH
Exile in Babylon

70 Years

OLD TESTAMENT

BETWEEN THE TESTAMENTS

NEW TESTAMENT

33AD
Pentecost, The New
Testament Church

33AD
Jesus Crucified

New Jerusalem
New Earth

STUDY 1
Warnings for God's People

Read the Introduction (page 5) and Background (pages 7–9).

A TIP
As we read through Zephaniah, it will be helpful to think of it as applying in different horizons of time and space. Think of the same prophecies having application in:

- Old Testament times, 640ish BC and locally to God's people (Judah) and the surrounding nations.
- New Testament times, the Early Church, and the Church now.
- Future times to come, worldwide for God's people and the nations (the world).

Have that at the back of your mind as you read.

Read Zephaniah 1:1

Q.1 What is a prophet?

A.1 God's messenger.
Zephaniah was a prophet who prophesied during the reign of King Josiah (640–609 BC). Zephaniah prophesied around the same time as Jeremiah, Nahum and Habakkuk.

Q.2 Have you ever heard a prophecy or been given one that was specifically for you?

A.2 Did it encourage you or change you in some way? Could you share it with the group? It builds the faith of others to hear a testimony of what God has said and done.

Q.3 Where does the passage tell us the authority for Zephaniah's message comes from? Whose words does he relay to the people?

A.3 His authority is from God. The first four words tell us that 'this is the word of the LORD'.

Q.4 In this first verse, we are given a potted family history of Zephaniah. This is fairly unique amongst the prophets; at most we're usually given one 'son of'. This extra detail could be significant. Why?

A.4 Zephaniah may well have had royal heritage. He was quite likely descended from good King Hezekiah (though we cannot be sure this is King Hezekiah, as there is no mention elsewhere of Hezekiah having other sons than Manasseh). A royal lineage would have given Zephaniah credibility and access to the ruling classes – even to the court of the king.

Q.5 Which other biblical characters also had access to the ruling classes?

A.5 For example, Moses was brought up in the court of Pharoah; Esther was married to the king; Nehemiah was cupbearer to the king. Each was uniquely situated for his/her mission.

Q.6 Is there something in your past or your present situation that makes you uniquely suited to what you are doing? Or are you uniquely suited to something else that you think God may be calling you to?

A.6 Consider your family, your environment, your upbringing, your education, your life experiences, your job, where you live, your contacts, your friends, your sphere of influence, hobbies, skills you have acquired, your current life circumstances.

Q.7 Look again at the names of Zephaniah's ancestors. What might all those names ending in 'iah' tell us?

A.7 Names ending in 'iah' refer to Yahweh (God).
Gedaliah = God is great.
Amariah = Promised by God.
Hezekiah = God strengthens.
Names often tell us much in the Bible, perhaps being clues to a person's mission or character.
Zephaniah means God hides or protects, and gives us a clue to the purpose of God's message.

Warning of coming destruction
Read Zephaniah 1:2–3

Q.8 Zephaniah's first prophecy certainly makes you sit up and take notice. What does this account of total destruction remind you of?

A.8a The Creation.
Note the order of destruction here is the opposite of the order of creation in Genesis. It's like a reversal or undoing of creation:

>GENESIS: Fish – Birds – Animals – Man.
>ZEPHANIAH: Man – Animals – Birds – Fish.

Additional reading: Genesis 1:20–26

A.8b The destruction of Noah's flood.
See what God says to Noah in Genesis 6:5–7. There are echoes in these first verses of Zephaniah 1:2–3 of a previous 'undoing' of creation. This passage is even fiercer than Noah's flood: every living thing will be wiped out.

One interpretation of these verses is that they are picture language, and the floodlike imagery reinforces the severity of what is about to happen to Judah. However, if a more literal interpretation is applied, then clearly these verses do not have their complete fulfilment in Zephaniah's time; the earth still exists today, with its animals, fish and birds. This fact gives us our first clue that Zephaniah's prophecy is not just about the immediate future for Jerusalem but is also about a future yet to come.

Q.9   What might this future event be?
Read Revelation 21:1–3.

A.9   There will ultimately be an end to the earth as we know it. God has promised us a new heaven and a new earth, where He will live among His cleansed and purified people.

Q.10   What does Noah's story show us about how God deals with the faithful few when the creatures of the earth are destroyed by the flood?

A.10   They are protected and kept safe (in the ark). The story of Noah and the flood can be found in Genesis 6:9–8:18.

Much of the Old Testament can be seen to have multiple layers of meaning:

- The history and remembrance of what God has done.
- The prophetic element – foreshadowings and prophesies about what God will do in the future.
- The overarching and repeating theme of salvation.

Q.11 Can you give an example of an Old Testament character or event that foreshadows Jesus or salvation?

A.11 Moses and the Passover foreshadow Jesus and salvation for God's people. Noah's ark foreshadows salvation for God's people. Both events show us God protecting His people from the wrath of His judgement.

The Lord's plan is to save you

Prophecy against Judah (God's people)
Read Zephaniah 1:4–6

Q.12 Straight out of the gate, we are given warnings of coming judgement for Judah (the southern kingdom). From history and from the rest of the Bible, we know that this came at the hands of the Babylonians, but nowhere does Zephaniah mention them by name. How might the people of Judah have had an inkling that it would be the Babylonians who would dispense God's justice?
Read Isaiah 39:1–8.

A.12 In the days of King Hezekiah, the king was warned by the prophet Isaiah that eventually the Babylonians would come and carry off his family and wealth to exile.

Q.13 Why can't God allow His people to go on unchecked in their bad behaviour?

A.13 God's people are meant to be an example (priests) to the world, demonstrating what it means to live under His law and blessing. If they have strayed so far that they are worse than the surrounding nations, then God is not likely to allow them to continue under His blessing. It would be quite the wrong sort of example. God's people were meant to bless the world, not lead them further astray.

Q.14 What does this have to say to us today? What warning might we take from this prophecy?

A.14 We cannot be fully under God's blessing if we are living in a way that is a bad example and contrary to all His laws. That would be the opposite of evangelism!

PERSONAL REFLECTION

Does this make you conscious of something in your own life? Are there ways you are living that are contrary to God's laws and guidelines?

Are there ways in which you are setting the wrong kind of example?

TAKE HOME POINTS:

- God wants to save His people. It has been His plan since before the days of Noah.

- We are meant to be an example to the world.

- God will not allow His people to remain in sin indefinitely.

- The Old Testament has more to say than just remembrance of history – there are multiple layers of meaning.

PRAYER

Father God,
Please help me to be the example to the world that I am meant to be. Please show me if there are areas of my life that sadden You.
Please help me to put these things right.
Thank You for Your great mercy and compassion.
Thank You for Your plan for salvation.
Thank You for Jesus.
Amen.

STUDY 2
False Gods

Prophecy against Judah (God's people)
Reread Zephaniah 1:4–6

Q.1 What is idolatry?

A.1 The worship of something other than God.

Verse 4 tells us that even the priests in Judah are idolatrous. The people are worshipping false gods.

Q.2 What do you know about Baal and Molek?

A.2 Baal and Molek were pagan gods. Baal worship occurs several times in the Old Testament; see for example the account of Elijah in 1 Kings 18:21–40. Baal required the sacrifice of children by fire. The name Baal means 'Lord'. There can only be one Lord for God's people.

King Solomon was led astray by pagan gods, including Molek, to whom he raised an altar near Jerusalem. The Bible tells us that God warned Solomon not to follow false gods, and in punishment for his sins, his heir would be deprived of ten of the twelve tribes of his kingdom.

Additional reading: 1 Kings 11:1–13

Molek was a god of the Ammonites. His name means king. The Bible is fierce in its denunciation of Molek, not only because of the sin of idolatry but also because of the terrible custom of sacrificing children by fire.

Additional reading: Jeremiah 32:32–35

God's people were tempted by pagan gods with their elaborate rituals, and priests who claimed that blood sacrifices and pagan rites could make their lives better.

Q.3 The people were worshipping false gods and sacrificing their children to them. What sort of things might we 'sacrifice to other gods' which are precious and belong to God?

A.3 Consider things like money and tithes, our time, our priorities, Sundays, worship, trust, devotion and love.

PERSONAL REFLECTION

Which false gods might you be inadvertently worshipping today?

Consider things you believe might make your life better in some way: money, celebrity, status, power, a dream you are pursuing. If God should bless you with these things, great! Be sure to thank Him. Just be careful that they don't corrupt you or lead you away from faithful obedience to God.

If you do not have these things, be happy with your lot, and don't look for ways to get them outside of God's boundaries.

What do you spend most of your time, thoughts and money on?

Q.4 What is a modern-day equivalent of worshipping the stars? What does God have to say in His law about worshipping the stars? Read Deuteronomy 4:19 and 17:2–5.

A.4 Horoscopes are a modern form of star worship, assigning power to a created object.
Israel had been warned not to worship the sun, moon and stars. The people of God in Zephaniah's time were playing fast and loose with their religion. Whilst calling themselves the people of God and outwardly observing some of the religious rituals, they were also worshipping other (false) gods and the stars.

Q.5 What would you say to someone who takes this 'New Age' view and claims all routes to God are equally valid? Is it all right to believe a bit of everything?

A.5 Jesus said, 'No one comes to the Father except through me.' (John 14:6 NIV). God said, through His prophet Isaiah, 'I am the LORD, and there is no other; apart from me there is no God.' (Isaiah 45:5 NIV). See also Exodus 20:1–3 and Exodus 34:14. God is a jealous God; we are to worship Him and Him only.

Only God is the LORD

Q.6 Do you live or work in an environment where political correctness and equality and diversity rules make it difficult to express these views? Can you share how you cope with this type of challenge?

A.6 Discuss and share any strategies you have found helpful. Perhaps equip yourself by learning some of the verses in answer 5. It's important to remain respectful of the views of others whilst not compromising your own faith.

Q.7 Why does it matter if we worship other gods as well as our God, the God of Abraham and Isaac?

A.7 If we worship false gods, we are putting our hope in something that's not real and not true. It's pointless. It's deceiving ourselves and potentially others too. It's offensive to the one true God.

Q.8 What stark warning does this passage give to those who turn back from following the Lord?

A.8 They will be cut off! (Some translations say 'destroyed'.)

Those in Zephaniah's time had originally worshipped God, but over time they turned away and began to worship other gods. Were the people in Zephaniah 1:6 just going through the motions of religion? Outwardly observing the rituals of the law but changing allegiance to suit the prevailing culture of idolatry? Their faith was compromised; they were no longer trusting in one God and the promised Messiah.

Q.9 Do you know people who have turned away from their apparent faith in Jesus? Do you think it's possible to totally lose your faith? Discuss.

Warning! This is a difficult issue with the potential for discussion to lead off at a tangent from the main point.

A.9 There are many passages in God's word that give us assurance that, if we truly believe and persevere till the end, then we shall be saved; that God will complete what He has started in us: e.g. John 6:39–40, Philippians 1:6.

We should consider that it is possible for some to learn to say and do the right things without having a true faith. If they then appear to fall away, one has to ask whether their faith was genuine. Equally, it would appear that some do fall away from faith and turn back to a life of sin – they harden their hearts to God and choose not to follow Him. They do not persevere to the end. This is not the same as temporary backsliding, which can happen to any of us in the peaks and troughs of life.

Additional readings: Hebrews 3:12–14 and 10:35–36

The take home message should be that we <u>can</u> have full assurance in Jesus if we persevere, and the gift of the Holy Spirit gives us confidence that our faith is genuine.
Read 2 Corinthians 1:21–22.

Additional readings: John 1:12 and John 5:24

PERSONAL REFLECTION

If you're not sure whether you are truly a Christian, please talk to your group leader or minister. If you know that you have just learned the right words to say but you're not sure what you really believe, then perhaps now is the time to share your concerns. The fact that you are concerned about this is a good sign! Read Jeremiah 29:13.

Would you say that you are currently in a spiritual peak or trough? Ask God to show you.

Is there anything that makes perseverance difficult for you? What dangers are there?

Ask your group members to pray for you.

Read Zephaniah 1:7–9

Q.10 Verse 7 says, 'The LORD has prepared a sacrifice; he has consecrated those he has invited.' (Zephaniah 1:7 NIV). What is the sacrifice God has prepared here and who are the invited guests?

A.10 The sacrifice is Judah; the invited guests, the Babylonians. 'Consecrated' in this case means the Babylonians were specially dedicated for a religious purpose – that is, to exact God's judgement on Judah.

Q.11 What do you think is the significance of 'foreign clothes' in verse 8?

A.11 These foreign clothes may refer to the clothes worn in the religious rituals of foreign gods.

Note: Special clothing is sometimes given by God as symbolic of certain roles and purposes. Priests in the Old Testament were given specific garments to wear. These clothes were set aside for use in the temple and were given by God to mark the priest out as separate to represent the people before Him. The priest was identifiable as holy before God so that he could enter God's presence without danger of death.

Q.12 What is the God-given New Testament parallel for these clothes? What did they foreshadow?
Read Isaiah 61:10.

A.12 God clothes us in righteousness by the blood of Jesus. These clothes of righteousness allow us to come directly into God's presence.

Those in Zephaniah's time were putting off their God-given clothes of righteousness and replacing them with the 'foreign' clothes of sin.

PERSONAL REFLECTION
Are there ways in which you are putting off your God-given clothes of righteousness and going back to the clothing of sin?

Q.13 Verse 9 says: 'On that day I will punish all who avoid stepping on the threshold' (Zephaniah 1:9 NIV).
Why is avoiding stepping on the threshold a problem? It seems harmless enough. Read 1 Samuel 5:1–5 where you will find an explanation for this seemingly strict approach.

A.13 Avoiding stepping on the threshold was a superstition that had arisen from the worship of a pagan god (Dagon).

Q.14 Which superstitions do you observe? Do you know where they originate?

A.14 Don't be tempted to assign power to things that are not of God, e.g. saying 'good luck', 'fingers crossed', 'touch wood', and the like. For instance, one widely held theory suggests that the tradition of touching wood originated from a pagan belief that trees were the homes of fairies and spirits. In contemporary culture, it's often used to avoid tempting fate.

Q.15 What does the tradition of 'fingers crossed' mean?

A.15 'Fingers crossed' has rather a muddled history and origins, some Christian, some pagan. Generally, when people use it today, it's for good luck, to hope a wish comes true, or to absolve them from telling some untruth (fingers crossed behind our backs somehow makes it all right to tell a lie). With such dubious and muddled origins and modern meanings, it is best avoided. It's likely to give the wrong impression even if your intentions are sincere.

Sayings like these may seem to be just figures of speech, traditions or folklore, but at the very least they set a bad example, and we know from Zephaniah 1:9 that God won't like them. Superstitions should be avoided.

Read Zephaniah 1:10–13

Q.16 In verse 12, God says He will 'search Jerusalem with lamps'. What does that mean?

A.16 There will be no hiding place; He will search every corner for every scrap of sin and idolatry.

Q.17 In which ways might you outwardly be following God whilst inwardly being far from Him?

A.17 We all have things like this in our lives that we try to keep hidden, while imagining that everyone else behaves perfectly. Aim to be consistent, remembering that God sees and knows. God wants us to behave in a godly way in all of life – at work and at home as well as in church.

Q.18 What will you resolve to try to do differently this
week? Is it something you could share with your group?

A.18 Pray for each other, perhaps splitting into prayer
triplets. Hold each other accountable and check next
week how your prayer triplet is getting on with this challenge.

Sharing challenges and struggles with your fellowship group is
part of what it means to be Church. Pray for each other and
support each other; be honest and vulnerable with one
another. Continue to pray for your group members throughout
the week and not just at your group meetings together.

Note: This might be a good time to remind the group that trust
depends on confidentiality.

PERSONAL REFLECTION

Are there areas in your life you think God won't see? Are there dark corners, things God might not like? Ask Him to show you.

Maybe it's drink or drugs, gambling, an unedifying television programme or book, or a fascination with the occult? Violent video games? Maybe it's small, maybe it's not. Either way, God may want to change it.

PRAYER

Oh Lord,
You see me, and You know me. Please forgive me for those areas of my life where I am not behaving in a godly way – living the outward show of faithfulness but not the inward reality.
Please help me to draw near to You. Help me, in Your mercy and compassion, to live with integrity and full of faith, so that I may be the person You made me to be.
Amen.

Verse 12 says:
'At that time I will search Jerusalem with lamps and punish those who are complacent, who are like wine left on its dregs, who think, "The LORD will do nothing, either good or bad."'
(Zephaniah 1:12 NIV)

Q.19 What is meant by 'wine left on its dregs'?

A.19 When wine is left a long time without decanting, the dregs from the fermenting process build up and accumulate. For a while, the dregs may serve some purpose in the wine's development, but if left too long they will make the whole batch undrinkable.

If the good wine is decanted, it will be unsettled but will be better for it: the dregs will then be thrown out. This term is symbolic of those in Judah who are complacent, thinking they don't need to improve or change. When God 'unsettles them' by exile, it is for the greater good – the bigger picture.

Q.20 Have you had times in your life when God unsettled you? What effect did it have? Did it move you on spiritually?

A.20 Consider times when it felt as though the rug was pulled out from under your feet. Perhaps a job came to an end; perhaps you were unwell or were forced to move home or church, or perhaps a relationship ended. How will you look with fresh eyes at this type of situation in the future? What might God be doing when He allows these things in our lives?

Read verse 12 again. The people of Judah were perhaps trusting in their status as the chosen people of God. Daily sacrifices may have been taking place, but they were complacent despite everything that was wrong in their lives and in society. They probably thought Jerusalem would be safe – that it would come under God's special protection. They may have thought themselves exempt from God's righteous anger. Yet they were denying the reality of a holy and powerful God, thinking He would 'do nothing'.

Q.21 In which areas of life might a person become complacent? Thinking the Lord will not act? Thinking 'the Lord will do nothing, either good or bad'? Suggest some typical examples.

A.21 Consider health, finances, living standards, employment, priorities, areas of behaviour, relationships.

Note: Comparing ourselves to the world and thinking 'we are not as bad as they are' is being complacent. We should instead compare ourselves to the true plumbline that is Jesus.

PERSONAL REFLECTION

Are there areas of your life that are detracting, or distracting you, from your relationship with God?

Don't imagine that He won't eventually intervene. Your relationship with Him is more important than all these other things. Your heavenly Father loves you too much to leave you in error or danger indefinitely.

Q.22 What are some areas in which a whole church may become complacent?

A.22 Consider congregation numbers, numbers of different church programmes, healthy finances, great worship team, nice buildings and sound doctrine.

Additional reading: Matthew 23:12

Q.23 What are some areas where a person might become complacent about his/her salvation?

A.23a Thinking sins don't matter because we are forgiven. Salvation should not be seen as some sort of licence to sin. God still hates sin just as He always did. We should be obedient out of love for Him; this matters to God. We should be obedient because sin has consequences; it harms us and it harms others. We should be obedient as a statement of faith; God is real and this is part of our calling.

A.23b Only real faith, real belief in Jesus will save you; not mere words or actions. Neither can we rely on the faith of those close to us – family members or friends.

As Church, we must be careful not to unwittingly deceive others into thinking they are saved by mere words of a particular form of prayer, by attending a church, or anything else other than belief in Jesus. We must be clear on the gospel message.

PERSONAL REFLECTION

Do you know how to lead another person to faith in Jesus? How to share the gospel message? What would you say? What resources would you find helpful?

TAKE HOME POINTS:

- Do not think that God won't act or can't see.

- Don't be complacent.

- Do not misuse what is precious to God.

- Be clear about the gospel message.

- Only God is the Lord.

- Superstitions should be avoided.

PRAYER

Dear Lord,

Please help me to see the areas where I am tempted to be complacent. Help me to be consistent in godly living, and show me if I have bad habits or if I inadvertently worship idols.

Lord, please enable me to overcome these things and live according to Your good plan for me.

Amen.

STUDY 3
The Day of the Lord

Read Zephaniah 1:14–18

Q.1 What is the Day of the Lord?

A.1 Is it Sunday? Is it Crucifixion day (Good Friday)? Is it the day of the Babylonian attack on Judah? Is it the day of Christ's return? Clue: it's not Sunday!

Here's where it's helpful to think of applications in different horizons of time and space. It's all the above (except Sunday).

In Zephaniah's time:
It speaks directly to Judah about their impending judgement and exile at the hands of the Babylonians.

In New Testament times:
It speaks of Christ's saving act on the cross. Judgement for God's people is satisfied by the sacrifice of Jesus.

For a future time yet to come:
It speaks of a final judgement and destruction of the earth; a time when Jesus will return. Fortunately for God's people, there is hope (chapter 2:3).

Note: The Day of the Lord has multiple fulfillments (see table on page 41) and is not necessarily just a day as we know it.

- The phrase 'the Day of the Lord' is used more by Zephaniah than any other prophet, even though the book is only three chapters long.

- The Day of the Lord is the time of enforcement of the provisions of the covenant.

- The Day of the Lord is the day when God will intervene.

If we skip through time again, we can see some common themes in the Day of the Lord, past and future.

- Covenantal curses are imposed. Judgement and destruction for God's enemies.

- Covenantal promises are fulfilled. Rescue for God's people.

- The establishment of God's Kingdom. A new chapter begins.

- What follows the Day is better than that which went before.

THE EVENT	CURSE IMPOSED	PROMISE FULFILLED
THE FLOOD	All living things on land destroyed by the flood.	God's faithful remnant saved in the Ark. Earth washed clean. A new start.
THE EXODUS	Egyptians destroyed.	God's people saved (The Passover). Set free from slavery.
THE CROSS	Jesus crucified in our place. Judgement satisfied.	Salvation for God's people. New Kingdom established.
THE FUTURE	Final judgement. Destruction for God's enemies.	God's people resurrected. New earth, new Jerusalem.

Q.2 Why does it matter that God's covenants are enforced?

A.2 God is a God of truth, a God of His word; He is faithful even when we are not. If He continued to bless a people who had gone so far off the rails, it would send the wrong message to the world about His trustworthiness and holiness.

The fact that God is faithful to His covenant conditions gives us security. We can also be sure about His promises being fulfilled to give us hope and a future.

If we can trust in His righteous judgement, we can also trust in salvation.

Additional reading: Jeremiah 29:11

Q.3 What might the clouds and darkness in verse 15 signify?

A.3a Darkness accompanies the Day of God's wrath. Read: Matthew 24:29, Matthew 27:45 and Joel 2:31.

A.3b Clouds often signify the presence of the Lord.

Q.4 Can you recall other times when the Lord's presence is accompanied by clouds?

A.4 God spoke to Moses at Mount Sinai: Exodus 19:9.
The glory of the Lord filled the Tabernacle: Exodus 40:34.
God's presence with the Israelites in the desert:
Exodus 40:36–38.
The Transfiguration: Matthew 17:5.
Jesus' return (the second coming): Matthew 24:30 and
Revelation 1:7.

Q.5 It was typical in Zephaniah's time for people to buy their way out of trouble, to pay off invading nations.
What does verse 18 tell us about relying on riches?

A.5 It's trusting in the wrong thing. Just like the idols, it won't save you. It can be gone in a blink.

Additional readings: 2 Kings 15:19–20 and 2 Kings 18:13–16

Q.6 What should our attitude to possessions be?

A.6 It's just 'stuff'; it doesn't hold any supernatural power.
Our only real security is in our identity as saved children of God. We should try to 'hold possessions lightly' – that is, acknowledge that we are merely custodians. Everything good that we have is a blessing from God. It can come, and it can go. We should not put our trust in it. We should be willing to let go of it if God asks us to.

Q.7 During Noah's flood, the earth's inhabitants were destroyed by water. How does Zephaniah tell us it will happen next time? Read Zephaniah 1:18.

A.7 The earth will ultimately be destroyed by fire.

Additional reading: 2 Peter 3:10–13

A call to repentance
Read Zephaniah 2:1–3

Q.8 What does the image of chaff represent?

A.8 This is an image from farming. The grain (the harvest) is sifted from the chaff (the loose bits of husk around the seed). The chaff is burned or blown away by the breeze whilst the good seed is kept. What is useless is discarded and removing it leaves the good seed uncontaminated, ready for use. In these verses, it is time to repent that is running out. The Day of the Lord will come suddenly; it will be unexpected. It will 'sweep on like chaff'.

Additional readings: Matthew 24:36–39 and 3:12

Q.9 God offers an escape route from His righteous wrath. What is it?

A.9 Seek the Lord, do what He commands, seek righteousness and humility. Or in New Testament terms: Seek God, do what He commands, trust in Jesus, ask for forgiveness, and humble ourselves before God.

Repent and Believe!

Note: The word 'perhaps' here (verse 3) should not be disconcerting for those who truly believe and trust in Jesus. It most likely referred to the immediate future for the people of Judah and Jerusalem. However, it serves as a useful reminder to us that salvation is a gift.

Q.10 How do we humble ourselves before God?

A.10 Have an appropriate fear of the Lord and acknowledge it's not all about you. Acknowledge God's power and sovereign hand on your life. Acknowledge that you are not God! You don't get to define what is right or wrong. Confess and repent of your sins, and be honest with God about your inadequacies. He knows them anyway. Admit to Him that you're not what you should be and ask Him to help you be what He wants you to be. Don't behave as though you have a right to blessing. Everything good that God gives is by His grace.

Q.11 What is grace?

A.11 Unearned, undeserved favour. A gift.

Note: To seek humility is more than to just be humble. It's a verb; it's active; it's something to be done.
To seek = To look for, to search out.

Q.12 What about humility before others? How can we actively be humble before other people? Suggest some practical examples.

A.12 Don't think of yourself more highly than others, but always put the needs and considerations of others first. Be ready to serve others. Treat others as you would like to be treated yourself.

> **PERSONAL REFLECTION**
>
> Could you make a conscious effort to behave with more humility? How?
>
> Are you conscious of things like status, titles, where you sit or who invites you to dinner?

Q.13 How can we be humble in our worship? Think about worship in church.

A.13 Do you ever comment on whether you liked the worship? It's important to remember that worship is not about you!

Perhaps better questions to ask are 'Did God like my worship today? Was it sincere, heartfelt, and humble? Did I recognise God's mighty power, His holiness, His worthiness of my praise?' Did you walk out of church changed? Did you allow God's word to change you? Were you humble enough to accept God's correction?

Note: Worship is not just singing. All of life should be an act of worship as we surrender ourselves daily to God's authority.

PERSONAL REFLECTION
Are you humble? Before God? Before others? What is motivating you? Is it pride, self-worth, ambition, self-importance, a need for validation, a need for respect, or a need to be noticed?

To actively seek humility is to put the needs, welfare, and value of others before your own. To actively avoid the limelight and give glory to someone else: to God. The less of me, the more of Him.

PRAYER
Dear Lord,
Please show me the areas where I am not humble. Show me where You would like me to actively seek humility. Please help me in this, Lord.
Amen.

Q.14 How can we know whether we are in the category of God's righteous people?

A.14 The Bible tells us that no one is righteous (Romans 3:10–12). We are all sinners, but as God's saved children we have the reassurance of the Holy Spirit that we are forgiven and made righteous in God's sight by the blood of Jesus. We are given the clothes of righteousness.

Additional readings: John 5:24 and Romans 8:1–2

Q.15 So does this mean we don't need to do anything else? How can we actively seek righteousness?

A.15 First and most importantly, we can make sure we are among God's saved children. We can ask God to show us where we need to change; we can listen to those inner promptings of the Holy Spirit and obey them. We can get familiar with God's laws and God's word.

Q.16 What will happen to God's faithful people on this future Day of the Lord?

A.16 Read Chapter 2:3 again. This is a key verse and a crucial part of Zephaniah's message:

> Seek God,
> seek righteousness and humility;
> perhaps you will be sheltered
> on the Day of His anger.

Zephaniah's very name gives a clue to his ministry: it means the Lord hides, or the Lord protects. God doesn't want us to be destroyed – He wants to protect us. To save us. To shelter us in the Day of His wrath.

Additional reading: Malachi 4:1–3

Q.17 In what way does God hide us now from His wrath? Read Colossians 3:3.

A.17 We are hidden with Christ (sometimes described as hidden in Christ).

Q.18 What does it mean to be hidden with Christ?

A.18 When God looks at us, He sees the new creation that is part of the body of Christ, united with Christ and justified (made righteous by the blood of Christ, sins paid for, justice already done). We are clothed in righteousness.

Q.19 Since we are made righteous, why do we still need to bother to obey God's laws?

A.19 Although we are forgiven, we have even more obligation to behave in a way that is pleasing to God and representative of God's people. Jesus said that He did not come to abolish the law, but to fulfil the law. We are thankful for God's grace because we can never be perfect. However, that doesn't mean we shouldn't try. In fact, we have even more responsibility now.

Luke 12:48b tells us that much will be required of those to whom much has been given.

We have a responsibility. We are priests/ambassadors to the world from the Kingdom of God.

As God's people we are supposed to:
- Show God to the world through our actions and the way we live.
- Demonstrate what it means to live under God's law and under God's blessing.
- Tell people how they can be put right with God; how they can have their sins forgiven; how they can have peace and reassurance about their eternal future.

Additional readings: Exodus 19:5–6 and 1 Peter 2:9–12

Q.20 How can we actively seek God?

A.20 By making time to spend with Him (quiet time). Praying and listening. Getting to know God's word (the Bible). Worship. Joining a church home group and attending church regularly.

PERSONAL REFLECTION

How much time do you spend actively seeking God?

What measures could you take to seek God more actively and which one measure will you focus on for the next few weeks? Set yourself a particular challenge or target.

PRAYER

Father God,

Please help me to find the time to actively seek You more. Please teach me to make space in my days and prompt me when I forget, and please encourage me as I try. I ask for safety from temptation, and perseverance when obstacles hinder my efforts. I long to be closer to You. To know You more each day. Thank You, Lord. Amen.

TAKE HOME POINTS:

- God is faithful to His covenant even when we are not.

- Actively seek God, seek righteousness, seek humility.

- God will hide His people in the day of His wrath. He doesn't want to destroy us – He wants to save us.

- We are meant to be priests to the world.

PRAYER

Thank You, Father, that You want to protect us in the day of Your wrath.
Thank You that we have the security of being hidden with Christ.
Thank You, Jesus, for what You have done for us.
Amen.

MAP

ASSYRIA

MEDITERRANEAN
SEA

ISRAEL

Ekron

AMMON

Ashdod
Ashkelon

Jerusalem

Gaza

MOAB

JUDAH

PHILISTIA

CUSH

STUDY 4

Judgement on the Nations

God put Israel in a strategic place so that they could be at a crossroads of multiple trade routes, with access to many nations and peoples. Thus they could be priests to the world, showing the nations what it means to live under God's law and God's blessing.

Q.1 What strategic places has God put you in?

A.1 Consider: where you work, where you live, clubs you belong to, the school gate, daily contacts, social media.

PERSONAL REFLECTION

How could you be a better priest to the world in the place where God has put you?

Consider whether you're setting a good example of Christian values and behaviour. What could you improve?

PERSONAL REFLECTION
Who could you pray for (bring before God) in the place where God has put you to serve Him as a priest to the world?

Q.2 Why did God regularly punish His people when they went astray?

A.2 Just as when a parent punishes a child – to correct and bring them back into line, to teach, to protect – so God's actions in this regard should be seen as an act of love. God disciplines His children because He loves them.

Additional reading: Hebrews 12:5–11

God wants His children to return to a state where He can bless them; where they can be in relationship with Him and be who they are meant to be: His ambassadors to the world.

Additional reading: Psalm 78:34–35

PERSONAL REFLECTION

Has there been a time when God disciplined you? What was the outcome? Are you grateful in hindsight?

Prophecy against Philistia
Read Zephaniah 2:4–7

Q.3 Where is Philistia?

A.3 Philistia in the time of Zephaniah was just WEST of Judah and south of Israel on the Mediterranean coast. The prophecies began with God's people in Judah and now move out to the neighbouring nations, starting with the nation of the Philistines.

Note: Gaza, Ashkelon, Ashdod and Ekron were the major Philistine cities of the time. The Kerethites were a Philistine clan of coastal-dwelling people who were living in Philistia. Other biblical references tell us they were once part of David's army. They may have originally come from Crete (being known as the sea peoples).

Q.4 Not only is the doom of God's enemies prophesied (motivation to repent) but there's something here for God's people too: a reason to be faithful, encouragement to stay in 'the remnant'. What is it? Reread verses 6–7.

A.4 God will restore His faithful remnant to the Promised Land. They will dwell in safety, they will have pasture, their fortunes will be restored. God Himself will care for them. The second part of this passage is about what will be handed over to the remnant of Judah.

This is another one of those occasions where it's helpful to think of different horizons of time and space. The prophecy also alludes to a future Day of the Lord, when the Promised Land will be restored to God's people.

When God made His covenant with Israel, He told them that, even if He banished them to distant lands, He would bring them back again. He would not break His covenant, even if they did. Read Jeremiah 29:10–14.

Additional reading: Deuteronomy 30:1–5

Q.5 Can you recall any other Bible passages where fortunes were restored to those 'returning from exile'?

A.5 See, for example, Job (exile from God's blessings): Job 42:12–13. The Israelites leaving Egypt: Exodus 12:35–38.

Prophecy against Moab and Ammon
Read Zephaniah 2:8–11

Q.6 Where are Moab and Ammon?

A.6 EAST of Judah.

Q.7 What do you know about the Moabites and Ammonites? Read Genesis 19:36–38.

A.7 Both nations were descendants of Lot, the result of incestuous relations with his daughters. These two nations became enemies of the descendants of Abraham, so, along with Edom (descended from Esau), were symbolic of God's enemies.

Q.8 Does this strike you as unfair for the generations of Moabites and Ammonites who will now suffer the fate brought on them by family history? What if we come from a long line of God's enemies? What would you tell someone who was worried by exactly this problem?

A.8 We who believe in Jesus are set free from any 'curse' that might be over the family or nation we belong to.

We are a new creation and part of a new family. In fact, we are now the 'seed of Abraham', with the blessings, inheritance and promises that go with that honoured and loved family.

Additional reading: Galatians 3:26–29

Q.9 Can you think of a Moabite who illustrates this point?

A.9 Ruth was a Moabite and became one of God's people by faith. She said to her mother-in-law, 'Your God is my God.' Ruth became one of the ancestors of Jesus.

The Moabite enemy of God's people was grafted into His family with hope and a future.

Additional readings: Ruth 1:16 and Matthew 1:1–6

Note: Even in Old Testament times, God made it clear that people would only be held accountable for their own sin and not the sins of their fathers (Ezekiel 18:19–20).

Prophecy against Cush
Read Zephaniah 2:12

Q.10 Where is Cush?

A.10 Egypt, Ethiopia and the upper Nile region. SOUTH of Judah.

Q.11 What might God's sword represent here?

A.11 God's weapon of the moment, the Babylonians. God often used other nations – nations who were God's enemies – to dispense judgement.

Prophecy against Assyria
Read Zephaniah 2:13–15

Q.12 What do you know about the Assyrians?

A.12 In 722 BC, the Assyrians conquered the northern kingdom of Israel and took many Israelites into captivity (the fall of the northern kingdom). Like the Babylonians, they were used by God to assert His purposes and judgement. They worshipped false gods. They ultimately get their comeuppance.

Q.13 Where is Assyria?

A.13 Assyria was northeast of Judah, but they tended to attack from the NORTH. So, we have covered the map of potential enemies of Judah: North, South, East and West. (Map: see page 54).

Q.14 What is so offensive in Nineveh's statement about itself in verse 15?

A.14 'She said to herself, "I am the one! And there is none besides me."'(Zephaniah 2:15 NIV).
This can be said of God and God alone. It even uses His name – 'I AM'. Read Isaiah 45:6b.

Additional reading: Exodus 3:13–15

Q.15 What does Zephaniah tell us about the fate of the 'nations' of the world?

A.15 Those in rebellion will not escape God's wrath. He will deal with the proud, the complacent, the unrepentant and those who choose not to seek Him.
Thank the Lord for Jesus and His plan for salvation.

Q.16 What impact does this have on our need to evangelise to those we care about? And to everyone else?

A.16 There is urgency. We have a responsibility. As Jude puts it, we might snatch them from the fire.

Additional reading: Luke 16:19–31

Q.17 What hope is there for the nations (the Gentiles)? Are they doomed? Read Isaiah 49:6.

A.17 They can be saved too if they repent and believe; if they turn to God. God's plan of Salvation is for everyone who turns to Him, Jew and Gentile alike.

PERSONAL REFLECTION

Do you know someone who needs to find Jesus? Is it someone God has given you compassion for? Someone you care about or someone you struggle with?

Make it a mission to pray for that person. Think how you could bring Jesus into a conversation. Could you invite them to a church or social event? Lend them a book? How could you be God's ambassador to that person?

TAKE HOME POINTS:

- We who are saved children of God are set free from generational curses.

- We are part of a new family, the 'seed of Abraham', with the blessings, inheritance and future promises that go with that honoured and loved family.

- God disciplines His children because He loves them.

- Evangelism is urgent!

PRAYER
Father God,
Thank You that I am set free from the actions and beliefs of those who have gone before. Thank You that I am part of Your beloved family. Please give me both a heart for someone else who needs to find this security, and the right words to say to them. Thank You, Lord.
Amen.

STUDY 5
The Future of Jerusalem

Read Zephaniah 3:1–5

Note how officials, rulers, prophets and priests have all failed to live up to God's standards.

Q.1 Why might they have been singled out?

A.1 They each had leadership responsibilities to the people, making their sins all the more treacherous.

Q.2 After the death of good King Josiah, Judah soon reverts to bad behaviour. How important is good leadership and why?

A.2 People rarely behave better than their leaders. If the leader sets a good example, the followers are more likely to behave well, living up to certain standards of conduct, integrity, and moral code. The reverse is also true: if the leader behaves badly, then the followers assume certain behaviours are acceptable, and standards fall.

Q.3 What lesson does this give to those with leadership responsibilities today?

A.3 Leaders have a moral responsibility; they will be held accountable. Take your responsibilities seriously.

Pray for your leaders: for church leaders, for those in authority over us, for the monarch and the government.

Q.4 In verse 4, we read that the priests 'profane the sanctuary and do violence to the law' (Zephaniah 3:4 NIV). In what ways do you think the people were profaning the sanctuary? Read Jeremiah 7:9–11.

A.4 The book of 2 Kings 21:4–7 also tells us that in an earlier generation, King Manasseh built altars to the stars in God's temple. He sacrificed his own son in the fire. He put the carved Asherah pole in the temple. He defiled the temple with false gods and evil practices.

Note: Asherah was the wife of a Canaanite god. Wooden poles in her honour were put near other pagan idols.

Q.5 In which ways might we profane (defile) the sanctuary today?

A.5 Consider things like trading in church, especially on Sundays; wearing inappropriate clothing, swearing and drunkenness; misuse of the building; taking advantage of the vulnerable. What about the communion of non-believers? Does your church hire out its buildings? What would it allow and not allow? Would it let other religions use them for a worship space? What about Halloween parties or a pagan AGM?

We often say that 'the Church' is the people and not the buildings, and that's true. But this doesn't mean that God doesn't care about the buildings being used in His name.

Q.6 What about the sanctuary of our bodies as temples of the Holy Spirit? How might we profane that kind of sanctuary?

A.6 Sin that involves our physical bodies: abuse of our bodies, mistreatment of them, or the bodies of others – for example, sex outside marriage, greed, alcohol abuse, drugs, committing violence, occult practices. Physical discipline is part of spiritual discipline.

Additional reading: 1 Corinthians 6:19–20

Q.7 What New Testament passage does this profaning of the sanctuary and violence to the law in Zephaniah 3:4 remind you of? Read Matthew 21:12–13.

A.7 Jesus overturning the tables of the moneychangers and the sellers in the temple.

Q.8 In what ways were those moneychangers and sellers in Matthew doing violence to the law?

A.8 They were neglecting the central principle of love for your neighbour by taking advantage of the poor, foreigners and the vulnerable. They were setting an example of ruthless, selfish greed in the very place that was the throne of God's presence. All this under the 'outer clothes' of respectability as temple workers.

Q.9 In what ways might we do violence to (inflict damage on) the law today?

A.9 Water it down, add to it, meld it to conform to the standards of society and the world, make it man's law and not God's law. We could decide not to obey it; to preach it inaccurately; misinterpret it; only talk about the bits that suit us; behave as though it doesn't exist; not teach it at all; mistranslate it. We might say things like, 'it was true then in its time, but it doesn't apply now'.

In Zephaniah's time, even the prophets were treacherous (verse 4). We can only imagine how, perhaps, they were charging people for what they wanted to hear instead of telling them what they needed to hear. Perhaps they were saying, 'God says...' to suit their own ends. Jeremiah 2:8 tells us that the priests didn't consult the Lord – the prophets even prophesied in the name of Baal.

Q.10 In contrast to the shortcomings of the people, what does God tell us about Himself (Zephaniah 3:5)?

A.10 He is righteous, He is just and He is consistent (morning by morning, every new day).

Q.11 Why is God's consistency both a bad and a good thing for the people of Judah?

A.11 If His judgements are consistent and reliable, so are His promises.

Read Zephaniah 3:6–8

God has clearly warned the people before about the consequences of their behaviour, but they haven't listened. They should have learned from the example of the destruction of other nations in the past; it should have served as a caution to them.

Q.12 Can you recall another city or country in the Old Testament that came under God's judgement?

A.12 For example, Sodom and Gomorrah (Genesis 19). Israel was exiled to Assyria in 722 BC.

Sometimes we suppress the still small voice of the Holy Spirit. We ignore the signs – that constant niggle that tells us we know we are doing wrong in the eyes of God. This passage reminds us again that God will not leave us to wallow in error indefinitely.

PERSONAL REFLECTION

Are there things in your life you know God is warning you about but which you consistently ignore? What prompting from the Holy Spirit do you need to pay attention to?

Read Zephaniah 3:9–13

'Then I will purify the lips of the peoples,
that all of them may call on the name of the Lord
and serve him shoulder to shoulder.' (Zephaniah 3:9 NIV)

Q.13 What do you think is meant by this verse?

A.13 Here again, we could look through time for multiple fulfilments. It's part imminent, part messianic prophecy, and part end times prophecy.

In Zephaniah's time:
The remnant of God's people would be exiled to a foreign land (Babylon) but in that exile, some would return to the true faith.

In New Testament times:
These verses foretell the gospel. The sacrifice of Jesus made it possible for God's faithful to call upon the name of the Lord in Spirit and in truth, and to serve Him shoulder to shoulder – Jew or Gentile – as one body, the Church, no matter where they came from. They would be purified and, as stated in verse 11, forgiven.

For a future yet to come:
Here we can only speculate, but this could refer to final refining when we are given resurrection bodies, free from worldly contamination and curse.

71

It could possibly mean that God will ultimately restore us to all speak the same language again, with a reversal of Babel (Genesis 11:1–9). Perhaps this is literal, perhaps not. It may mean we will be of one accord in the way we speak and the things we agree on. Perhaps we will speak many languages, but all be able to understand one another. We see a foretaste of this in Acts 2:1–11 on the day of Pentecost, maybe to have its complete fulfilment in the future.

Additional reading: Revelation 19:5–7

There are many things we can know for certain, but there are aspects of theology or biblical interpretation that we cannot know for certain. We should avoid dogmatic arguments about such things and, in humility, admit that God alone knows the answers.

Note: Zephaniah 3:12–13 tells us that a remnant of Judah will be left behind: the meek and the humble. The Babylonians typically left a certain number behind as local workers, mainly from the poorer members of society.

Jeremiah tells us that the remnant who were exiled to Babylon were those God regarded as good. The people left behind would ultimately be destroyed.

Additional reading: Jeremiah 24:1–10

Q.14 In verse 13, Zephaniah prophesies an ultimate end to fear, lies and deceit. When did these sins first creep into the human experience? Read Genesis 3:8–10 and Genesis 4:8–9.

A.14 The Fall. Adam and Eve were afraid when they heard God in the garden. Cain lied to God about killing his brother.

Fear, lies and deceit were never meant to be part of life. In the New Jerusalem, God will ultimately put things back to the way they were designed to be.

TAKE HOME POINTS:

- Leaders have responsibilities; they will be held accountable. We should pray for our leaders.

- We should handle the law carefully and faithfully.

- We should respect the sanctuary that is God's house (both the physical building and the spiritual temple that is our body).

- God is consistent, the same yesterday, today, forever.

- We must not ignore God's loving correction or the promptings of the Holy Spirit.

PRAYER
Father God,
Please bless our leaders. Please give them wisdom and integrity for the sake of us all.
Father, help us to handle Your law with diligence. Be the voice always behind us saying, 'This is the way – walk in it.'
Amen.

STUDY 6
Prophecy Fulfilled

Read Zephaniah 3:14–17

Once again, we can think in different levels of meaning for Zephaniah's time, for the New Testament Church, and for a future yet to come.

Q.1 What might the meanings be (verses 15 and 17)...

In Zephaniah's time?

For the New Testament Church?

For a future yet to come?

A.1 **In Zephaniah's time:**
After the exile, the people would eventually return to Jerusalem in the Promised Land.

For the New Testament Church:
The Lord your God is with you: **Immanuel God with us.**
He has removed your punishment: **Forgiven.**
He has turned back the enemy: **Death is conquered.**
He is mighty to save: **Salvation by the blood of Jesus.**

For a future yet to come:
God's people return to the Promised Land. The New Jerusalem, the city where these things will have their fulfilment. God will dwell with His people forever.

Q.2 Verse 17 says God rejoices over His people with singing. What image does this suggest for you?

A.2 This is how I imagine it:
God takes you in His arms; He rocks you gently as He sings a lullaby of peace over you, rejoicing in His heart. He is full of love for you as He speaks of plans for your future.

The feasts fulfilled
Read Zephaniah 3:18–20

Q.3 What are the appointed feasts (some translations call them festivals)? Name them. What do you know about them?

A.3 The feasts were given for remembrance of events past, and to celebrate particular annual events. But they also have a prophetic element for the future.

See the following tables.

SPRING FEASTS

OLD TESTAMENT	PROPHECY FULFILLED
PASSOVER: Remembers the Passover of Exodus 12.	**CRUCIFIXION:** The sacrificial Passover Lamb – Jesus.
FIRST FRUITS: Celebrates the first fruits of the harvest.	**RESURRECTION:** Jesus, the first fruits of those to be resurrected.
PENTECOST (WEEKS): Remembers the giving of the law. Celebrates the gathering in of the harvest.	**PENTECOST:** The giving of the Holy Spirit. The Early Church begins.

The time between the spring and autumn feasts is most likely fulfilled by this present era of the New Testament Church.

If we need more evidence of these connections, the spring feasts had their New Testament fulfilment on the precise dates of the Old Testament feasts.

The Crucifixion was on the feast of Passover (Passover began in the evening and went on into the next day).

The Resurrection was on First Fruits (Jesus was the first fruits of those who are to be resurrected – see 1 Corinthians 15:20).

Pentecost, on the feast of Pentecost, celebrates the coming of the Holy Spirit. Traditionally the date the law was given to Moses, now this is the day the written law is superseded by the law of the Spirit, and when the first of the harvest becomes the New Testament Church.

> **Additional readings: Acts 2:1–4 and Acts 2:41**

With the benefit of hindsight, it's easy to match up the timing of the spring feasts. The timing and linking of the autumn feasts is far more speculative. We don't know the when or the exact detail of these future fulfilments, but we can see the symbolism and foreshadowing. We can live in the light of what we are privileged to know. In Colossians 2:16–17 Paul tells us that the feasts were a shadow of what was to come.

AUTUMN FEASTS

OLD TESTAMENT	WHAT WE KNOW SO FAR
TRUMPETS: A gathering of God's people before the Lord for His favour. The beginning of judgement. A time to get right with God – a time for repentance and reflection.	**THE MINISTRIES OF JESUS AND OF JOHN THE BAPTIST:** The whole world will ultimately come before the Lord to be judged.
DAY OF ATONEMENT: The high priest enters the Holy of Holies and makes atonement for the sins of the people with a blood sacrifice. A time to repent and ask for forgiveness.	**CRUCIFIXION:** Jesus opened the way for God's children into the Holy of Holies; into God's presence. Once for all atonement for our sins. There will ultimately be a day of God's wrath for the world.
TABERNACLES: Celebrates the autumn harvest. The people gathered to Jerusalem and lived in tents or booths, symbolising God dwelling with His people.	**IMMANUEL:** God with us. God's people will be gathered to The New Jerusalem, where God will dwell with His people forever. **Revelation 21:1–3.**

In Old Testament times, the people didn't know the when or the how of the coming Messiah. But although they didn't know the details, they had the signs, the prophecies and the foreshadowing. They knew that there would be a Messiah from the line of David. They could trust in the Promised One.

Q.4   What lessons might we take from the autumn feasts?

A.4   A day of judgement will come for the whole world. Check yourself, repent, get right with God. Live in the light of Christ's return. Share the gospel.

Additional readings: Matthew 25:13 and James 1:22

PERSONAL REFLECTION

Give yourself a spiritual audit:

Are you living in the light of Christ's return? If you knew He was going to return in a fortnight, what would you change? What would your priorities be?

Q.5 What lesson does verse 19 have for those who oppress others?

A.5 God Himself will deal with them. A sobering thought.

Q.6 What promises does God give here to His people (verses 19–20)?

A.6 He will rescue the lame. The exiles will eventually return home; their fortunes will be restored. They will have honour and praise.

Note: God always brings His children back to the Promised Land from exile (Deuteronomy 30:4–5).

Q.7 What eventually happened to Jerusalem in Zephaniah's time?

A.7 Ultimately, the people in Zephaniah's time didn't listen for long. They slipped back into their old ways despite God sending them more prophets (Jeremiah and Habakkuk). Read 2 Chronicles 36:17–21.

King Nebuchadnezzar and his Babylonian army routed Jerusalem. Many people were killed, young and old. The temple was looted of all its gold and silver treasures and then set on fire; the wall of Jerusalem was demolished. The Babylonians burned the palaces and destroyed everything of value. The people who were left were carried off into exile to Babylon.

Note: 1 and 2 Chronicles are rarely read in churches today. They don't tend to feature in the lectionary which sets the readings for churches on a three-year cycle, designed to cover the majority of the Bible. These two books contain great insight into the history of God's people and help to set things into context.

Q.8 What was the significance of seventy years of exile?

A.8 In 2 Chronicles 36:21, we're told that the land enjoyed its sabbath rests. In the law, the people were commanded to give the land a sabbath rest every seven years; to leave the land fallow. In their many years of rebellion, they had not been following this and many other rules. Now God was giving the land the seventy years of sabbath rest it was owed. The exile was execution of justice even for the land.

Additional reading: Leviticus 25:1–7

We could also read seventy in terms of biblical symbols:
7 x 10 = completeness.
3 score years and 10 = a biblical lifetime.

Note: Seventy years of exile was prophesied by Jeremiah (Jeremiah 29:10).

Q.9 What happened after seventy years of exile in Babylon had passed? Read Ezra 1:1–11.

A.9 Before the seventy years were up, God moved the heart of the King of Persia to rebuild the temple in Jerusalem. He allowed some of the exiles to return for this purpose. In addition, Cyrus the King provided the finance and returned the articles that had originally been looted from the temple.

The new temple was finally dedicated in 516 BC, seventy years after the destruction of the old temple in 586 BC (Ezra 6:15–16).

The priests were installed (Ezra 6:18), and everything was ready for the return of a larger group of exiles.

In Ezra 7:11–13, we are told how King Artaxerxes, now King of Persia, decrees that anyone who wants to is free to return home.

Q.10 What does the destruction and rebuilding of the temple foreshadow? Read John 2:18–22.

A.10 The death and resurrection of Jesus.

Recap of Zephaniah

Q.11 What does the book of Zephaniah tell us about God's overarching plan for His people?

A.11 If we cast our minds back to the images of the dregs of wine and the chaff, we can see that God's people were being sifted and decanted, cleansed and purified of all that would contaminate.

God's purpose has been to refine and restore His people to a holy state. He wants to protect and save them; to bring them back into relationship with Him, into His blessing and into His presence, so that they can be priests to the world again as they were always meant to be.

God urges His people to repent and seek Him. He plans to save them from their rightful judgement; to protect them on the day of His wrath.

PERSONAL REFLECTION

In what ways can you see God's overarching plan for your life?

Are there ways in which you are fighting against God? Struggling to go a different way?

If God's plan for you is to protect and save you, to refine you to be the best that you can be as His ambassador to the world, does this throw any new light on your area of struggle?

Q.12 What does Zephaniah tell us about what God requires of us (chapter 2:3)?

A.12 Seek Him, seek righteousness and humility, and do what He commands. Repent and believe.

Q.13 What hope does God give for our future safety?

A.13 Our salvation is assured when we believe and trust in Jesus. We do not need to fear the wrath and judgement of God – the debt for our sin is paid. We are hidden by God, hidden with Christ. Alleluia!

Additional reading: Psalm 91:1–2

TAKE HOME POINTS:

- God will ultimately make good on His warnings.

- Get right with God.

- God's faithful people will always be restored to the Promised Land (gathered home).

- Our deliverance is not in doubt if we are 'in Christ'.

- Prophecy requires a response; it's not just empty, pointless words. Seek the Lord! Seek humility, seek righteousness. Do as He commands.

PRAYER

Dear Lord,
Please help me to get right with You. To pursue humility and righteousness. To seek You every day.
Thank You for Your plan to save me and bring me into Your blessings. Thank You for Jesus.
And thank You that my deliverance is not in doubt – that I am hidden with Christ.
Amen.

ZEPHANIAH

Zephaniah is like a snapshot from the story of God's people
and His salvation plan for them.

Chapter 1
The undoing of creation.
The wicked will perish and
there will be nowhere for them to hide.
THE DAY OF THE LORD WILL COME,
with trumpet and battle cry.
There will be blood poured out.
The earth will be consumed by fire.

Chapter 2
SEEK THE LORD.
SEEK RIGHTEOUSNESS AND HUMILITY.
DO WHAT HE COMMANDS.
HE WILL SHELTER YOU.
The nations will be judged.

Chapter 3
There is a future hope for God's people.
There will be purification,
forgiveness, restoration and rejoicing:
your punishment removed.
THE LORD IS WITH YOU.
Your fortune and honour restored.
GOD HIMSELF IS YOUR RESCUER.
He will gather you home.

CONCLUSION

How will the book of Zephaniah make you read the Bible from now on? Will you look with fresh eyes for echoes of the past and promises for the future? For multiple layers, connections between the Old Testament and the New? For signposts to Jesus and to a future yet to come?

Additional reading: Jeremiah 33:3

About the Author

S K Featherstone led a large church home group for over ten years and was employed on a busy church staff team for just over thirteen years.

Now living in the English countryside and part of a rural parish, life is more relaxed and has allowed the time to study, and to prepare 'ready to use' Bible study notes for other busy small group leaders.

Printed in Great Britain
by Amazon

47289246R00056